my first fruits
in hebrew

translated by Josephine Simple

polyglot kids

תַּפּוּחַ

tah-PU-akh

apple

אֲגָס

ah-GASS

pear

עָנָב

ah-NAV

grape

תְּאֵנָה

teh-NAH

fig

תּוּת

TOOT

mulberry

שָׁזִיף

shah-ZEEF

plum

דּוּבְדְּבָן

doov-deh-VAN

cherry

אֲפַרְסֵק

afar-SECK

peach

רִמּוֹן

ree-MON

pomegranate

מֶלוֹן

meh-LON

melon

© 2025 by Polyglot Kids Books / World Poetry Books
Photography © 2025 by Sebastian Fröhlich

Series editors: Peter Constantine & Hannes Schumacher
Translated into Hebrew by Josephine Simple
Photography: Sebastian Fröhlich
Design: Hannes Schumacher & Sebastian Fröhlich
ISBN: 978-1-967821-04-4

Polyglot Kids Books is an imprint of World Poetry Books, Inc. New York.

www.ingramcontent.com/pod-product-compliance
Lightning Source LLC
Chambersburg PA
CBHW061355010526
44107CB00012B/943